GIOTTO AND HIS CONTEMPORARIES

by ENZO CARLI

TRANSLATED BY SUSAN BELLAMY

CROWN PUBLISHERS INC. ▪ NEW YORK 1958

Printed in Italy ▪ Istituto Italiano d'Arti Grafiche ▪ Bergamo
All Rights reserved

GIOTTO

DUCCIO

SIMONE MARTINI

PIETRO AND AMBROGIO LORENZETTI

THE GREAT MASTERS OF THE FOURTEENTH CENTURY IN TUSCANY

A great process of rebirth and development had, since the second half of the Thirteenth Century, captured all phases of Italian culture, from poetry to legal science, from theology and philosophy to medicine, from historical research to literature and art. The revival gave Italy in a short time the pre-eminence that had heretofore belonged to France, and enabled her, to quote Salvatorelli, « to create the first great temporal culture since the decline of the antique ». Painting matured rather late in this development, in fact painting was perhaps the last creative activity to proclaim the novelty of its own spirit and to take in hand its own fate.

Restricting this observation to the arts, one customarily considers as the first expression of this new style in painting, the frescos in the church in Assisi in which the history of St. Francis is depicted. This work can hardly have been created before the first years of the Fourteenth Century. At that time Nicolo Pisano, the founder of the new trend in sculpture, was already dead more than ten years. In addition, a basic change in architectural style was beginning; Gothic elements from beyond the Alps became more and more unified which, in the Romanesque epoch, led to many varied local architectural traditions. It is not easy to explain this retardation, however small, in painting in comparison with the other arts; we can merely point to the persistent vitality of the Greek and Byzantine styles. This vitality manifested itself in the variety of its style and received new inspiration from the recovery of its past Hellenistic sources, which in the Twelfth and Thirteenth Centuries had brought about a second Golden Age. To this must be added the great reverence and the almost sacred and immutable character of the very wide iconography which arose from the varied demands of the Christian cult and the pictorial spread of the Christian dogma. (It must, however, be remembered that the new style in painting found its first most daring and most perfect expression in the cycles of frescos by Giotto and his successors, while on the other hand mural-painting, an essentially Italian art form, had had no opportunity to develop under the influence and the contributions of its predecessors in the North.) These contributions were of less importance in painting than in the other arts and consisted almost exclusively of certain autochthon creation and practically free from Nordic influences. But in order to develop in the form which made it world-famous, namely in fresco painting, it had to wait until architecture had developed to the point where it was able to take in the new style and to develop it further. It is in fact hard to conceive that the History of St. Francis in Assissi or the cycles in the Scrovegni Chapel in Padua could be removed and separated from the buildings for which they were created. They are all related to the architectural peculiarities of these places, in the closest intimacy of spirit, culture and form. The slight delay in the development of the new style in painting is, however, more than made up for by the speed and the decisiveness with which painting freed itself from the Greek manner despite having to pass through the most diversified trends in order to become independent. This was due, above all, to the unusual talent and the strongly individualistic character of its founders and first champions, and the great esteem which they enjoyed among their contemporaries. Whereas in the feudal countries — France, Spain, Germany — at that time, and for a long time thereafter the greatest artists disappeared in the anonymous mass of vassals, artisans and workmen of lower rank, in Italy a Giotto, a Duccio di Buoninsegna, a Simone Martini were considered among the most prominent citizens of their community. They were also sought after and honored outside of their own country, were the favorites of the people, and stood on terms of the greatest intimacy and friendship with the most eminent and the most powerful men of their times. It is true that preceding centuries had honored and praised the architects of their cathedrals and the sculptors who decorated them, but the works of painters had found but little praise among their contemporaries, and only toward the end of the Thirteenth Century and the beginning of the Fourteenth Century did conditions change, and then they went to the other extreme. Neither Dante, nor Petrarch, nor Boccaccio as much as mentioned the sculptors of their day although Niccolo and Giovanni Pisano, Arnolfo di Cambio and Andrea di Pontedera were their contemporaries. But Dante expends great praise on Giotto and Cimabue; Petrarch was a friend and enthusiastic admirer of Simone Martini, and the heros of some of the picaresque novels of Boccaccio are three Florentine painters.

>*Credette Cimabue nella pittura*
>*Tener lo campo, ed ora ha Giotto il grido,*
>*Si che la fama di colui oscura.....*

>Cimabue thought to hold the field,
>As painter, but everybody praises Giotto's name
>So that he obscures the fame of the other.

This famous triplet from the eleventh Canto of Dante's *Purgatorio* is the first living testimony that we have of the new social status of the Tuscan painters of the Fourteenth Century From the contrast between the « latest » — the *dernier cri* — Giotto and the then « obscured » fame of Cimabue, and from the fact that such a seemingly ideal rivalry between teacher and pupil could interest a scientist, philosopher and poet like Dante, we can deduce that painting among the varied forms of human activity, had achieved, for the first time since antiquity, a dignity and a fame that permitted it to attain an equal status with poetry.

This happened not only in Florence; in the nearby Siena the whole populace met, together with the clergy and the authorities, in the studio of a painter and saluted with enthusiasm his masterpiece, the famous *Madonna in her glory* by Duccio di Buoninsegna. And next to the passion for glory of Cimabue, his ambition to remain the first, to maintain the field, appeared the proud self-confidence with which Duccio di Buoninsegna praised his own merits. Relinquishing his anonymity and in the place of the traditional humble invocation *orate pro eo*, the master who had painted her so perfectly, seemed to announce his claim to special intercession of the Virgin with the inscription *Sis Ducio vita - te quis depinxit ita*, which he placed at the feet of the Mother of God in his most important work.

If in the history of painting of the Twelfth and Thirteenth Centuries a few stylistically strong dominant personalities are distinguishable, it is nevertheless often necessary to label them with conventional designations like Master of Amagni, Master of the Magdalen etc. Only at the beginning of the Fourteenth Century did there appear a row of creative individuals, and the development assumes a monographic character. By this we do not mean to say that the artists detached themselves from each other; on the contrary, the more they stepped forward and distinguished themselves from each other, the more did the movement which they had started, and which had influenced the taste and the general culture of their time, contribute to the development of regular local tradition. In this way only does the designation *schools* achieve general critical validity.

Whereas, however, Italian sculpture of the Gothic epoch arises from one root only, the glorious studio of the Pisanos, form its branches, the new popular style of painting shows from its inception two clearly distinguishable trends or schools which in the first decades of the Fourteenth Century achieve their fullest expression and their most marked individuality: the school of Florence and that of Siena.

It is astonishing that two cities such as Florence and Siena which lie in the same district, not more than a hundred kilometers from each other, should develop two diverse styles, styles so rich and fruitful in the artistic solutions of painter's problems that during the whole of the Fourteenth Century they inspired not only the artistic culture of all Italy but even influenced a considerable portion of the whole European continent. These traditions differ in their cultural premises and in their stylistic achievements and each is forcibly the expression of a different and sometimes opposing attitude toward reality.

One was aware of this as early as the Eighteenth Century when for instance a learned scholar like the Padre della Valle wrote: « Florence seems to me the home of thinkers, Siena of poets; one can bring forth philosophers, the other artists full of life and imagination ». If we overlook a certain superficiality of this critical judgement — for the Florentine painters certainly were no less poets than those of Siena — these words express in a pregnant manner the contrast of the two styles. The Florentines in their constant search for plastic effects and for strict and clear formal definitions, seem dominated by a clear and logical spirit, whereas the paintings of the Siena masters with their predilection for color and their sophisticated love of line show a nature that is turned toward the mythical, the phantasmic. Their love of line is a free and pure expression of a musical and decorative sensitivity.

The essence of both schools arrived at their perfect expression, at their accomplished synthesis in the works of a few great masters who were active in the first decades of the Fourteenth Century. These are Giotto in Florence, Duccio di Buoninsegna, Simone Martini and the brothers Pietro and Ambrogio Lorenzetti in Siena. They had many pupils; efficient and exceptional painters continued their work, but not one was oble to equal these masters or add to their once expressed artistic achievement a significant new word. And notwithstanding the many successful investigations, discoveries and new appraisals of modern criticism we must even today accord to these five names the summit of the artistic fame of the whole Fourteenth Century.

GIOTTO

Giotto di Bondone was born 1266 or 1267 in Colle di Vospignano in the Mugello valley. His parents were simple peasants who sent their son to guard the sheep at pasture. Cimabue watched him as he drew a sheep on a piece of stone; surprised at the precocious talent of the boy, the artist took him along to Florence where he kept him as his pupil. This is Vasari's version, but although art critics usually consider this tale pure invention, probability speaks for its truth, at least it mirrors the facts whose confirmation one seeks in vain in the more authentic but drier accounts in the archives.

The education of Giotto by Cimabue has never been questioned, nor has the wholly new and revolutionary process by which Giotto let himself be inspired by nature so that he was able to take reality as his model, even if that reality was only a modest sheep; ultimately one accepted the story of his lowly and rural descent.

This latter circumstance is of interest because it explains certain aspects of his art. We know little about the social origins of the artists of those days, but the little we know proves that the most prominent among them were of urban, and frequently of wealthy origin, if they did not actually belong to the aristocracy. Cimabue, for instance, who like Dante studied at the Dominican school in Santa Maria Novella, was a scion of the lower Florentine aristocracy; Pietro Cavallini, Giotto's other mentor, descended from the noble Roman house of Carroni of the Rione Monti; similarly the Sienese Duccio di Buoninsegna, whose ancestors owned houses and properties in Rione Camporeggi. As for the cultured and sensitive Simone Martini, who associated with courtiers and scholars on an intimate footing, and who was wealthy at an early age, it is unthinkable that he was of lowly descent; of Ambrogio Lorenzetti we know through Della Valle that his household was « rather that of a noble and a philosopher than that of an artist. » The peasant descent of Giotto, on the other hand, is evidenced by the bold, unprejudiced character of his genius which ignored sophisticated finesse, and the gay, country-like, untrammeled style of many of his compositions with backgrounds of the harsh Tuscan landscape; also the fresh concrete quality of his imagination. Many of his character traits also point in this direction. For instance, like many country people, he was a careful steward of his possessions; although not avaricious, he was certainly not disdainful of money and always eager to profit from his own endeavors and to increase his earnings. The same Giotto who was to crown St. Francis, the *poverello* of Assisi, with his most beautiful wreath, wrote a Song of Poverty, merely to ridicule it in jest as the origin of all sin and unhappiness.

Although as we have shown, the tradition that Giotto had been a pupil of Cimabue has been universally accepted, the question of the beginnings of this painter remains one of the most uncertain and most debated questions in the history of art. The first works that can be allocated to him with any certainty belong to an already fairly advanced stage of his development; it is not in Florence where he was raised and where he spent his whole youth but in Assisi, in this varied cultural *milieu*, that we can recognize for the first time a style of painting that is so new, so serene and so original that we can unquestionably see his personality in it.

Cimabue was, of course, the dominating personality in the group of masters who, during the last quarter of the Thirteenth Century, worked on the decorative paintings in the basilica in Assisi and remained so until the *Histories of the life of St. Francis* in the basement of the nave were begun. As however Cimabue and his assistants had completed the Histories in the transept, the scenes from the Old and New Testaments were started in the top sections of the nave, and here we note besides the Florentine studios which were still supervised by Cimabue, a number of Umbrian and Roman painters in whose work we can distinguish the new trends. They are clearly differentiated from the harsh, solemn Byzantine style of Cimabue and stand under the sign of a festive gay classicism, a school whose founder and most important exponent in Rome was Pietro Cavallini. It is improbable that Cavallini himself worked in Assisi nor do we know anything about the relations of Giotto to the great Roman master; Cavallini's sedate and majestic ideals of beauty as well as his strong and plastic style of painting with its rich and carefully differentiated color mixtures show a clear first step toward the style of Giotto. It is significant that the critique has designated repeatedly the upper bands of these murals in which the Florentine tradition of Cimabue and the Roman tradition of Cavallini become a unity, as the only place in which we can recognize the art of Giotto. Even if his authorship in some scenes like the two *Blessings of Joseph* is questionable, it is certain that among the *Histories of the New Testament* the tragic and powerful *Pietà* is already in every respect a work worthy of the great master.

The question whether Giotto painted the twenty-eight *Histories from the life of St. Francis* which form the lowest band, has been much debated, unjustly we believe, although many see in them the first revelation of Giotto's genius.

The tradition that they were painted by Giotto is not specifically proven by contemporary documents, but it goes back a long time and can refer to creditable evidence. We read, for instance, in Vasari that Giotto worked on them at a time when Giovanni de Muro was General of the Order of St. Francis — which means after 1296. As early as the Eighteenth Century it was discovered that not all scenes were painted by the same hand; the daring care of modern critique started with them and expanded its doubts and reservations to the whole cycle. A polemic started which reached its climax in 1912. In that year a German scholar, F. Rintelen, published a monograph in which he, with unquestionable sagacity, interpreted the basic aspects of Giotto's art but plainly stated that Giotto never participated in the decorations of the basilica in Assissi. This bold theory of Rintelen which he elaborated with great scholarship and with dialectic dexterity found, and still finds, many adherents, primarily among critics outside of Italy. Besides a long and uninterrupted literary tradition, enough historical and stylistic arguments speak against his thesis, but even it it were not the case it would be difficult to imagine at the side of Giotto a second equally important and pioneering personality who showed the same profound and living humanity and who was able to express itself in the same forceful and original language. This is the reason we must emphasize the unquestioned, unmistakable originality of the *Histories of St. Francis* in Assissi. Giotto certainly had assistants, especially in the last three quarters which, as is now univerally admitted, were executed by the Florentine Master of St. Cecilia. It is also established that more humble, possibly local artists participated in the work but it remains certain that the conception as a whole belongs to Giotto himself; the whole concept of the cycle has not only artistic importance but constitutes a decisive step on the path of the entire occidental culture.

For the first time a religious theme, the description and glorification of the life of a personality of recent history, which was already surrounded by a mythical and serene lustre, was depicted with human sympathy and intimate directness without thereby creating a realistic chronicle or a colored anecdotal illustration. The Histories of Giotto are free of liturgical or festive additions without, however, losing themselves in external descriptions; they depict the truly eternal spiritual content of the Franciscan experience and include it fearlessly in the cycle of human existence, in the live and permanent course of human emotions.

The depiction of the events and the impulses of the soul are expressed in the visible eloquence of human gestures. These gain in the simplicity of their natural impulses that physical concreteness which gives them a power of conviction and expression which remains valid for the taste of all time. In this way a profound truth speaks from these figures; with it is closely connected a constant striving after plastic power in the depiction of the figures as well as a new treatment of the landscapes and the special figurations. These elements are no longer abstractly stylized or selected with symbolic intent but are depicted without prejudice in free and manifold reality. Landscape and architecture, on the other hand, are not restricted, notwithstanding their careful characterization, to the role of mere scenarios of the episodes shown; they rather adapt themselves to the figures, form, as it were, their own structure, their own profiles, their special rhythm after the figures and so attempt to summarize the action in its most important moments and to emphasize the deeper dramatic and ethical meaning of the events. We see for instance how in the *Renunciation of Earthly Goods* the incompatibilty of the two disputing groups is symbolized by the silent opposition of the two buildings; or how in the *Donation of the Cloak*, the spiritual superiority of the figure of the Saint is expressed less through its halo than through its position at the intersection of the lines of the landscape background; how in the *Sermon to the Birds* the big tree on the right leans over as if to support the soft flight of the bird and as if it too would like to approach in order to listen to the words of the Saint; how in the glorious *Wonder of the Source* the mountain tops, rising from the light-flooded rocky steps, mirror and emphasize the rising fervent prayer of St. Francis.

A few years only separate the completion of the Franciscan cycle in Assissi, or rather the departure of Giotto who left the execution of the last Histories to his pupils, from the beginning of a far wider and more engaging work, the decoration of the Arena Chapel in Padua. Between about the years 1297 or 1298 and 1303 the master lived in Rome where he executed the often renovated mosaic with the *Ship of St. Peter* in the columned hall of the Dome of St. Peter; of the original of this the two tondos with two Angel's heads of massive construction and strong color tones recalling Cavallini remain (in the Museum of St. Peters and the Museum of the Palazzo Venezia). He also painted at that time in San Giovanni di Laterano a fresco with the *Annunciation of the Jubilee Year*, a few parts of the original painting of which . were discovered in the past few years under the countless repaintings which had made it completely unrecognizable. Above all from this time, and not of a later epoch, as many suppose, must probably be dated the first and most famous altar painting of Giotto, his *Madonna and Child* which was at first in the Ognissanti Church in Florence and is now in the Uffizi.

The Virgin is strictly presented *en face* but the slight turn of the body suffices to let us feel the granite-hard plasticity of the block in which she is placed so that she, as if driven by a mysterious power, seems to come nearer to the viewer. Her figure is enveloped in such intensified, superhuman loneliness that at a first glance we do not realize that she is surrounded by fourteen Angels and Saints; her figure is upheld by the delicate side-wings of the throne which are not too weak to bear so heavy a load, but are there to achieve a linear and spacial connection with the surrounding figures. In this way a unified and organic impression is created which contributes no little to the great magic of this « definite » picture in which the highest pictorial problems of the time find their synthesis; from the endeavors for a plastic picturization, the heritage of the Romanic sculptural tradition, to the new unlocking of space, the architectural achievement of Arnolfo di Cambio.

The Arena or Scrovegni Chapel was built in 1303 by Enrico Scrovegno, a noble from Padua who wished through the munificence of this pious donation to atone for the evil life of his father, Reginaldo Scrovegno, whom Dante had placed among the usurers in the Seventh Cycle of the inferno. The architecture of the chapel is of great simplicity; the exterior is without decoration, the interior seems to be created especially to house frescos and bring them out to best advantage; we might suppose that Giotto himself participated in the planning of its form and proportions. In any event the decoration must have been carried out with unusual speed as the dedication of the chapel took place on March 25, 1305. It is possible that at that time the monochrome figures of the *Virtue* and *Sins* in the zone of the base as well as the large depiction of *Judgement Day* on the inner wall of the façade were not yet accomplished, but they were certainly completed by March 25 of the following year.

When Giotto undertook this work which constitutes a milestone in the whole history of Italian painting, he was not yet forty years of age, but he already had at his command the whole power and maturity of his years of mastership. In the frescos in Assissi the language of Giotto, in its lightning-like revelation and its rhapsodic expression, still spoke through forms of compository arrangements and divisions of space which recalled youthful brittleness; in the cycle of the Arena Chapel the language is more decisive and stricter in the compactness of its plastic statements; it merges and unites more strongly with the composition and the coloration. Thus the tone of the story-telling becomes more serious and more concise; it loses its restlessness and achieves a deeper, more intimate, almost fatalistic impressiveness.

The themes of the Padua frescos from the life of the Madonna and the Life and the Passion of Christ as well as the *Judgement Day* look back on an ancient and glorious iconographic tradition, and yet Giotto immersed himself in them with fresh emotion and interpreted them as a novel, marvelous and consoling message in which the human personality, now fully responsible for its actions, and therefore no longer abstractly conceived, becomes intimately connected with God and achieves a novel dignity of the highest order. And so simple events of every-day life, which Giotto does not hesitate to include in his episodes, affect the senses with solemnity as do religious happenings and human gestures, even if they are fashioned after the most humble and most commonplace reality; they speak with a nobility which has nothing rhetorical or pedantic in it but which adds to the emotions thus expressed, something venerable. Thus the composed sorrow of *Joakim with the Shephards* appears humanly touching but constitutes, above all, the symbol of Christian renunciation. In the same way the gentle embrace of the married couple in the *Meeting at the Golden Gates* in which the two figures merge into one mass depicts more than the expression of tender feelings; their shy modesty lifts them into a higher sphere. Let us see and admire under the same aspect of spiritual absorption and stylistic perfection the thoughtful resignation of the Virgin in the *Annunciation*, the reverent tenderness of the *Magi before the Christ Child*, the veil of meditative melancholy over the impassive profile of the Virgin in the *Flight into Egypt* and above all the gay majesty, the superhuman spiritual command as it always appears in the traits of Christ, especially in His eyes, whether He performs the *Miracle of the Wine* in the *Wedding at Canaan*, awakens *Lazarus* or looks piercingly at *Judas*, where the silent reproach of His eyes seems here to perforate the whole figure of the treacherous disciple.

As we progress from the upper bands which were the first to be painted to the scenes of the lower bands, we can identify a gradual change in Giotto's style which testifies again to the inexhaustible versatility of his genius. In fact in the last pictures space appears less thinned out, there is more air circulating between the figures and groups and the composition seeks to enrich itself through a greater variety of pictorial planes. The planes become more numerous and correspond to the converging main lines which run across or into the background. The figures appear less massive and less dependent on the planes of the background; they move more freely and with a restlessness which reminds us of the best traits of the Assissi cycle without, however, any brittleness. The best example of this greater variety in the composition is the glorious *Bewailing of the Dead Christ* where the equality of the masses, the appropriateness of the rhythms and the carefully thought-out intervals achieve in a solemn *legato* the touching drama of the event, a theme which has its dramatic and spiritual center in the corpse of Christ.

Even more clearly can we see the development in Giotto's art in the *Episodes from the Life of the Evangelist John and John the Baptist* and the *Histories from the Life of St. Francis* which were created as frescos perhaps after 1317, in the chapels of the Peruzzi and Barti families in Santa Croce in Florence. They are the last assured testimonials to the activity of the master and although the many restorations of the past century when they were freed of the whitewash of the Sixteenth Century, do not admit an exact critical examination, we can yet detect the new spirit of the composition which expresses itself in a solemn and classical monumental rhythm. The power of the cycles of Assisi and Padua is slightly weakened in these works and the action strives rather toward a slow and grave unfolding like a strict liturgical hymn than a converging toward a dramatic center.

Giotto lived, wandering and working, in many Italian cities; he visited Rimini and Verona, Padua and Milan but unfortunately little of the activity of his late years has come down to us. A few paintings, which carry his name, are now unanimously considered works of the studio and the frescos are all destroyed. He also occupied himself with sculptural and architectural works; about the year 1334 he sketched the plans for the *campanile* of Santa Maria del Fiore in Florence; perhaps he also furnished models for several relief-like paintings on the pedestal. Death which surprised him on January 8, 1337, did not let him see the completion of this work; its name, however, *il campanil di Giotto*, was to assure for him a popularity which surpasses even the fame of his genius as a painter.

GIOTTO (about 1266-
1337) - St. Francis
Honored by a Man of
the People. (Detail). -
Assissi, Basilica
di San Francesco

GIOTTO (about 1266-1337) - St. Francis Gives his Cloak to a Beggar. - Assissi, Basilica di San Francesco

GIOTTO (about 1266-
1337) - St. Francis Gives
his Cloak to a Beggar.
(Detail). - Assissi,
Basilica di San Francesco

19

GIOTTO (about 1266-1337) - St. Francis Renounces all Earthly Goods. - Assissi, Basilica di San Francesco

GIOTTO (about 1266-1337) - The Dream of Pope Innocence III. - Assissi, Basilica di San Francesco

GIOTTO (about 1266-1337) - The Vision of the Chariot of Fire. - Assissi, Basilica di San Francesco

GIOTTO (about 1266-1337) - St. Francis Expels the Demons from the City of Arezzo. - Assissi, Basilica di San Francesco

GIOTTO (about 1266-
1337) - The Miracle of
the Man Dying of Thirst.
Assissi, Basilica
di San Francesco

24

GIOTTO (about 1266-1337) - The Sermon of the Doves. - Assissi, Basilica di San Francesco

25

GIOTTO (about 1266-1337) - The Madonna in Her Glory. Florence, Uffizi

26

GIOTTO (about 1266-1337) - Joakim with the Herdsmen. - Padua, Scrovegni Chapel

GIOTTO (about 1266-1337) - Joakim's Dream. - Padua, Scrovegni Chapel

GIOTTO (about 1266-1337)
Joakim's Dream. (Detail).
Padua, Scrovegni Chapel

29

GIOTTO (about 1266-1337) - The Meeting of Anna and Joakim at the Golden Gates. - Padua, Scrovegni Chapel

GIOTTO (about 1266-
1337) - Annunciation.
(Detail). - Padua,
Scrovegni Chapel

31

GIOTTO (about 1266-1337) - The Adoration of the Magi. (Detail). Padua, Scrovegni Chapel

32

GIOTTO (about 1266-1337) - The Adoration of the Magi. (Detail). Padua, Scrovegni Chapel

GIOTTO (about 1266-1337) - Presentation of Jesus in the Temple. - Padua, Scrovegni Chapel

GIOTTO (about 1266-1337) - The Flight into Egypt. - Padua, Scrovegni Chapel

GIOTTO (about 1266-1337) - The Flight into Egypt. (Detail).
Padua, Scrovegni Chapel

GIOTTO (about 1266-
1337) - The Wedding
in Canaan. (Detail).
Padua, Scrovegni Chapel

GIOTTO (about 1266-1̶
The Resurrection
Lazarus. (Detail).
Padua, Scrovegni Ch̶

38

GIOTTO (about 1266-1337) - The Resurrection of Lazarus. (Detail). - Padua, Scrovegni Chapel

GIOTTO (about 1266-
1337) - The Foot
Washing. (Detail).
Padua, Scrovegni Chapel

40

GIOTTO (about 1266-1337) - The Betrayal of Judas. - Padua, Scrovegni Chapel

GIOTTO (about 1266-1337) - The Descent from the Cross. - Padua, Scrovegni Chapel

DUCCIO DI BUONINSEGNA

The Sienese master, Duccio di Buoninsegna differs from Giotto not only by his temperament, and his taste, but also by his education and his culture. Notwithstanding his training by Cimabue and his other experiences as expressed in his paintings, Giotto seemed to have derived his creative energy directly from the perception of concrete reality, from his consideration of the passions, the emotions of humanity and also the simple, clear outlines of his Tuscan landscape which he discovered anew with an open mind and an unbiased eye. Duccio, on the other hand, had his roots in a soil that had been fed by a century old venerable artistic tradition and was unusually receptive to refined cultural stimuli. He did not use, (as Cennino Gennini said in his famous words regarding Giotto, « the Latin instead of the Greek style of painting » but continued to express himself, after a fashion, in the Greek manner. Nevertheless he was no less « modern » than the Master from the Mugello Valley. One might even conclude that his greatest historical achievement was to have, in a wonderful way, modernized the old Greek style.

This style had distinguished itself during the second half of the Thirteenth Century through its special delicacy and discrimination. This applies especially to the coloration, which remained one of the most enchanting virtues of Sienese painting. When Duccio started modestly in the years 1278 and 1279 to decorate for the community document chests and lids for financial registers, there arose from the studios of prominent Sienese painters whose names we can no longer identify, works like the two side altars with St. Peter and St. John and the histories of their lives, which are now in the State Museum of Siena. These works which in their elegant compositions and charming coloration can be considered masterpieces of Byzantine Post-Hellenism in Tuscany, must by their magic have strongly influenced Duccio nor did he forget it when he came in contact with Cimabue. We do not know whether this occurred in Florence or in Assissi, whether he was a pupil, a collaborator or an assistant.

Duccio was probably indebted to Cimabue for the first important commission, of which we have any knowledge. It was a big panel for the Brotherhood of the Choral Singers of Santa Maria Novella in Florence. This work can be identified with the so-called *Madonna Rucellai* which was formerly in Santa Maria Novella and is now in the Uffizi. This commission is dated 1285; that a foreign, and especially a Sienese painter was entrusted with so important an order, proves that he had achieved high mastery and also a certain reputation, which must have pleased Cimabue, who dominated the artistic affairs of his native city. Duccio's style must have been not too far from Cimabue's stylistic demands. In fact the *Madonna Rucellai* was considered for several centuries a work by Cimabue until the written commission to Duccio was discovered. However, along with undeniable suggestions of the style of Cimabue, this painting contains definite elements which refer to Siena or are characteristic of Duccio; this is especially noticeable in the light and airy composition with the six Angels who float gracefully in the middle of the painting, the clear and refined scale of the colors and finally the charming and decorative linear direction which in the sinuous flow of the seam of the gown can almost be called Gothic. The continued intensification of these pictorial elements of different origins, their enrichment through ever closer blending, is shown in several works from the years 1285 to 1308; the composition and color go back to Oriental-Byzantine traditions, the linear style, however, to occidental Gothic-French style. Among these works the small, select *Madonna dei Francescani* from the Sienese Museum should not be forgotten. Finally the stylistic development of Duccio achieved its culmination in a masterpiece which assured his fame and epitomized his whole artistic culture.

This work is the *Maestà*, the depiction of Maria as Queen, venerated by the patrons of the city, which he painted between 1308 and 1311 for the high altar of the Dome in Siena where it remained until the beginning of the Eighteenth Century. It consisted originally of a great panel, painted on both sides, with a predella and crowning pictorial panels. In 1795 front and back were separated and they can be seen in this condition in the Museum of the Dome of Siena. Predella and crowning were likewise separated; of these sections several remained in the Dome Museum, while others went to foreign countries and can be found in the National Gallery in London, the National Gallery in Washington and the Frick Museum in New York; others have been lost.

The front consists of a single composition, dedicated to the praise of the Virgin; she sits on a throne surrounded by her heavenly court, Saints and Angels, while the four Patron Saints of Siena, Ansano, Creszencio, Savino and Vittore kneel at her feet. The strict order in which these figures are arranged gives their apolline beauty a superhuman dignity. Their facial expressions are absorbed as if in a dream, in a condition of fervent ecstasy and profound bliss, and through this the Byzantine principle of symmetry and repetition loses its officious stiffness and formality to rise to the highest sphere of poetry. The Virgin, herself, is portrayed queenly, and at the same time motherly; her monumental proportions and the golden and marble splendor that surrounds her are loosened and humanized by the gentle inclination of her head and the penetrating charm of her glance.

The back of the panel is divided into twenty-six sections which, connecting with the *Histories of Childhood* and the *Life of Christ* in the predella, contain the *Passion of Christ*. In the panels which Wimperger and Engels divided into half-figures which originally contained the *Coronation*, we see the *Appearance of Christ* in the forty days after the Resurrection and the last events in the *Life of Maria* after the death of Christ.

Two or three of these scenes in their exceptional clarity, their fine execution and their truly glorious color would suffice to convince us of the greatness of Duccio and to give us exhaustive information about the problems that his art poses. In all of them the old iconographic schemata of Byzantine tradition are completely re-stated with a clear knowledge of the stylistic significance and the poetic function of the elements which form them. The result of this purification is not only an exceptional formal elegance, but from the perfect balance of the figures and their serene accordance with the landscape and their surroundings, arises the refined lyrical tone of Duccio's style which differs considerably from the vision of Giotto, in fact is its very opposite. He is able through a gesture, a figure, an episode to awaken a mysterious echo and to raise the representation beyond the limits of the painting and beyond the participation in the events, as we see them in Giotto's histories, into a region of unreal and magical, dream-like dimensions. In this way he achieves the timeless condition of suspense and of pure representation. In the story of the *Passion*, for instance, the repeated appearance of Christ achieves a meaning, notwithstanding His manifold actions and gowns; as an innocent victim before Pilate, with denuded, martyred limbs in the hour of the Crucifixion, in a gold embroidered gown after the Resurrection. This meaning does not arise from the necessity to point to Him as the true and sole protagonist of the drama; His figure is the center of all the elements of the composition and impresses itself on our consciousness with a force which transcends the conditions of the representation. It is a presence, a message which draws the sensibility of the viewer from an immutable and unattainable heaven.

It is in any event astonishing that Duccio should succeed in arriving at a sphere so lofty that it appears rarified by his imagination, and at the same time to remain true to the text of the Gospels, and to fulfill the task of making this text clear and comprehensible. For this he uses the most appropriate scenery and never disregards the clearest direction of the landscape and the architecture or even the inner decoration. Thus the historical conditions of each episode are clarified; but above all, the representation achieves a unique poetical magic. We admire, for instance, how Duccio understood the necessity of varying from scene to scene, the traditional conventional form which the Byzantine style employed to present rocks and mountains.

Let us restrict ourselves to some of the episodes which we have selected in this work: In the *Adoration of the Magi*, the mountains are conceived in a single mass, the contours of which accord with the hanging roof of the hut and act as a background which shuts it off from the rest of the world. In the *Flight into Egypt*, they mount as a horizontal wall of rock which glows in the far background as if struck by the setting sun, while in the foreground the figures emerge as in a classical relief. In the *Prayer on the Mount of Olives*, the light-flooded mountain slope is split and so creates a cavity in the shadow which emphasizes the secrecy and intimacy of Christ's prayer. In the *Women at the Grave*, the mountain tops recede in perspective and emphasize the shy retreat of the pious visitors before the glowing appearance of the Angel. In *Noli me Tangere*, the rocks surround the valley in a half-circle in which the words of the Resurrected seem to echo.

Great splendor is shown in the interiors of the delicately tinted walls as well as the panelling, the timber work of the ceilings, the rafters, carved of light-colored wood, the half-open doors and even the common-place articles as in the *Foot Washing*, the black boots of the Apostles and the towel, negligently thrown over a horizontal rod. We see in these the intimate poetry of every-day things as we shall see them with other Sienese artists above all with Pietro Lorenzetti and the painters of the Fifteenth Century.

In the works of Duccio we see announced the characteristics and the destiny of Sienese painting, the soft intoxication which made the numerous creations of religious themes popular, the fine rhythm of the compositions, the predeliction for lively and thought-out colors, which goes back to Byzantine style, and the Gothic feeling for musical lineation. With its persistant reminiscence of the venerable iconography of the miniatures in the menologies and the evangelistaries of the Orient the episodes of the *Maestà* of Duccio seem to bring to a conclusion a widespread artistic culture that had persisted for many centuries. They announce in fact a wholly new style of painting the radiation of which, though limited in time and space, was to create no lesser masterpieces.

DUCCIO DI BUONINSEGNA (known from 1278 to 1317/18) - The Madonna in Her Glory. - Siena, Museum of the Dome

DUCCIO DI BUONINSEGNA (known from 1278 to 1317/18) - The Adoration of the Magi. - Siena, Museum of the Dome

DUCCIO DI BUONINSEGNA (known from 1278 to 1317/18) - The Flight into Egypt. - Siena, Museum of the Dome

DUCCIO DI BUONINSEGNA (known from 1278 to 1317/18) - The Wedding of Canaan. - Siena, Museum of the Dome

DUCCIO DI BUONINSEGNA (known from 1278 to 1317/18) - The Miraculous Draught of Fishes.
Siena, Museum of the Dome

DUCCIO DI BUONINSEGNA
(known from 1278 to 1317/18)
The Entry into Jerusalem
Siena, Museum of the Dome

DUCCIO DI BUONINSEGNA (known from 1278 to 1317/18) - The Foot Washing. - Siena, Museum of the Dome

DUCCIO DI BUONINSEGNA (known from 1278 to 1317/18) - The Prayer in the Garden of Gethsemane
Siena, Museum of the Dome

DUCCIO DI BUONINSEGNA (known from 1278 to 1317/18) - The Kiss of Judas. - Siena, Museum of the Dome

DUCCIO DI BUONINSEGNA (known from 1278 to 1317/18) - The Women at the Grave. - Siena, Museum of the Dome

DUCCIO DI BUONINSEGNA (known from 1278 to 1317/18) - Noli me Tangere ! - Siena, Museum of the Dome

DUCCIO DI BUONINSEGNA (known from 1278 to 1317/18) - The Walk to Emmaus. - Siena, Museum of the Dome

DUCCIO DI BUONINSEGNA (known from 1278 to 1317/18) - The Apparition of Jesus at the Closed Doors.
Siena, Museum of the Dome

DUCCIO DI BUONINSEGNA (known from 1278 to 1317/18) - The Doubting Thomas. - Siena, Museum of the Dome

SIMONE MARTINI (about 1285-1344) - The Madonna in Her Glory. - Siena, Palazzo Pubblico

62

SIMONE MARTINI

Duccio di Buoninsegna died in the year 1318, only a few years after his *Maestà* was solemnly installed on the high altar of the Dome; at that time, however, another no less wonderful *Maestà* covered the wall of honor in the big hall of the Siena *Palazzo Pubblico*; Simone Martini had painted it as a fresco in 1315.

The *Maestà* in the *Palazzo Pubblico* is the first authentic work of Simone that has come down to us; but in it we can already distinguish the personality of the artist, also the basic stylistic and spiritual difference which separates this fresco from its model, the fresco by Duccio in which the Saints, freer, airier and livelier, surround the Madonna who sits on a fragile openwork throne painted in the Gothic manner. The mood of a mystical play which Duccio had expressed through the ecstatic immobility of the adoring multitude, arranged in strictly hieratic order, is more human in Simone's work. It seems to exhaust itself in the concrete expression of a festive and courtly event which, however, is not free of a certain refined mundane grace. The unusual elegance of the figures is most striking, as well as their rhythmic and relaxed pose which emphasizes the musical continuity of their design. One might well maintain that this harmonious flow of their contours decides the structure of their bodies which lose their massiveness, and surrounding the throne of the Virgin; they are slightly bent forward like stalks of grain, moved by a gust of wind. It is above all the joy in the drawing which is blended, as with Duccio, though even more perfect, with a choice of rare colors, which raises the pictures of Martini above any naturalism and moves them into a world of fantasy, determined by a strict and crystal-clear imagination. This pleasure in design, which matured in the purest and most impressive creations of Gothic art, from the miniatures of the Paris school to the sculpture of Giovanni Pisano, becomes, with Simone Martini, not only the basic element of his creations but the true source of his inspiration. In it his essential being is expressed, and in the scanning of his inner rhythm he becomes aware of himself. This rhythm takes everything unto itself, attracts it, like an irresistible call of the blood. For this reason and on account of this continual intensification, Martini's lyrical tone hardly varies, even in intensity, with all the different themes which he seeks to portray, the sacred as well as the profane; whether they correspond to the aspirations of a renewed piety of the laity and the *bourgeoisie* like his *Maestà* (which the Municipal Council of Siena decided to install in the place of honor in the town hall), or whether they renew archaic forms, like his *Polyptych* which he painted four years later, in 1319, for the Dominicans in Pisa, now in the Pisa National Museum. It remained the same whether the artist was commissioned by one of the most sophisticated courts of Europe to depict the virtues of a Saint of royal blood as in the fine panel painting *St. Louis of Toulouse Crowning Robert of Anjou*, (now in the *Museo Nazionale* in Naples) or whether he depicted a touching story of child-like miracles over the tomb of an eremite who had just died in the surroundings of Siena, like his *Votive Tablet for St. Agostino Novello* in San Agostino Novello in Siena. This chronicle of little children who fell from a balcony out of their cradle or were bitten by a dog, is raised to the realm of purest poetry.

The altar picture for San Agostino Novello, which a short time ago was judged to be the work of Martini, and of which we reproduce here one of the most charming portions, must be considered an exception among the works of this master. This once he was forced to interest himself in the fate of the children, the artisans, the little townsfolk, the seamstresses in their homes, which populated, in the Middle Ages, the narrow, neglected streets of Siena, overshadowed by loggias and galleries. From these lowly trivial events he gathered poetical themes, but as a rule his imagination sought other models. It roamed through an aristocratic world of fairytales with anaemic female beauties and incorporeal apparitions, to re-invoke, not without a touch of nostalgia, the glory of by-gone generations of knightly heroes, *sans peur et sans reproche*. In his *Madonna in Her Glory*, of the *Palazzo Pubblico*, the traditional veneration of the people of Siena for their heavenly patroness had taken on a wordly and chivalrous tone; it showed in the graceful flowers, in the magnificence of the throne, which was roofed with a silken baldachin like the tribune of a tourney, and also in the verses of the dedication which adorned the frame of the painting. After this work, the frescos which, fifteen years later, decorated the Chapel of San Francesco in Assissi with the *Life of St. Martin Of Tours*, were his most important creation.

Here the theme inspired the artist to depict the world that he loved in a most effective and suggestive manner. The scenes in which Simone, with detailed and unusual documentary precision, represented episodes from the knightly and warlike life of the Saint, are unforgettable. Especially fine are the scenes of the *Saint Giving His Gown to a Beggar* and the scenes where he is knighted and when he leaves the service as a warrior. In the first picture St. Martin appears as an elegant young man with curly blond hair, wielding as a weapon a sharp sword and mounting an unruly white steed; in the second picture the artist does not omit the smallest detail of the ceremony, and attention is drawn to both the Saint and the Emperor, the two main characters, as well as to the other figures; the armigers who attach the spurs, the jugglers and musicians in their multicolored gowns, who sing their songs to the accompaniment of a mandolin and a curious double flute, the pages, who tend the cap and the falcon. In the third episode the imperial tent with its collection of spears, shields, helmets, and tents behind a rock wall, create an atmosphere which accords with the place and the action. And yet, notwithstanding the abundance and the realism of these details, embodying historical reality, the whole episode breathes the mood of a timeless fairytale. The mood persists, and when Simone has to undertake a topical happening and has to depict a character that he certainly knew personally, who did not carry the reputation of sainthood, did not present a particularly attractive appearance and did not show unusual mental gifts, it was no easy task to idealize him. This happened when he, after 1328, was called upon to glorify the victory won by Guido Riccio da Fogliano, an honorable captain in the services of Siena, over the rebellious castles Montemassi and Sassoforte, on the wall facing his *Madonna in Her Glory* in the hall of the *Palazzo Pubblico*. It was a rather modest police action which would have been completely forgotten by the historians if it had not given rise to this masterpiece. Guido Riccio is depicted riding in the midst of stark, naked rocks, between palisades, trenches and other warlike preparations; his body is covered by a handsome uniform cloak, but appears fat and stocky; the face is commonplace and without charm. But between this realistic portrait and the abstract contours of the landscape, the metaphysical loneliness of the castles, the shields, the floating banners, a wonderful harmony arises; through the elegant play of the contours, the heraldic division on the horse blanket with the floating modeling of the hem, this portrait of an ugly soldier and adventurer loses its materialness and enters the fairytale region of dreams.

Here we see again the capacity for stylistic abstraction, the same musical design which reaches one of its climaxes in the famous *Annunciation* which was painted in 1333 for the Dome in Siena and is now in the Uffizi.

This painting of Martini might be called his most Gothic, as the lines here reach the utmost limits of melodic absoluteness and depict merely through the force of their rise, their bending, their repeated incorporeal appearance, limbs and faces which seem transparent like holy wafers and weightless gestures which, in the great luminosity of the golden background, seem to multiply. The point seems to have been reached where these lines appear to descend in the arbitrariness of the purely ornamental. But Martini's feeling for moderation, and the wonderful harmony between the inner emotions and the free play of the artistic means — line and color — avoid this danger. The artist, therefore, gives us in this *Annunciation* of the Uffizi not only a new enchanting work of art, but also the most difficult, almost acrobatic example of his stylistic mastery.

In 1339 Simone Martini went to Avignon, at the invitation of Pope Benedict III, and there he died in 1344. As we have already mentioned, his knowledge of French Gothic art contributed largely to the original formation of his style; during his short but intensive activity in Avignon he repaid far more than he had received. This is proven less by the remainders of his frescos on the portal of Notre-Dame-de-Dons which are now bleached and eroded by the sun and the winds of the Provence, but by the charming little picture in Gothic style, *The Return of the Christ Child to the Temple*, now in the Liverpool Museum, and a dramatic *Polyptych*, which has now been divided between the Museums of Berlin, Antwerp and the Louvre. Not only painting and the art of the miniature of Provence remained faithful throughout the whole Fourteenth Century to his teachings, but also the art of Bohemia, Catalonia and Flanders; they all showed for a long time living traces of his artistic methods. One can rightfully state that Simone Martini was the first truly European manifestation in the history of Italian art.

SIMONE MARTINI (about 1285-1344) - St. Martin Gives his Cloak to a Begger. - Assissi, Basilica di San Francesco

SIMONE MARTINI (about 1344) - St. Martin in Kni
Armor
Assissi, Basilica di San Fran

SIMONE MARTINI (about 1285-
) - St. Martin in Knightly
Armor. (Detail).
Assisi, Basilica di San Francesco

69

SIMONE MARTINI (about 1285-1344) - St. Martin before the Emperor. - Assissi, Basilica di San Francesco

SIMONE MARTINI
(about 1285-1344)
St. Martin before the Emperor.
(Detail). - Assissi,
Basilica di San Francesco

71

SIMONE MARTINI
(about 1285-1344)
St. Francis. - Assissi
Basilica di San Francesco

SIMONE MARTINI
(about 1285-1344)
St. Clare. - Assissi,
Basilica di San Francesco

73

SIMONE MARTINI
(about 1285-1344)
The Annunciation: the
Angels. - Assissi,
(Basilica di San Francesco)

SIMONE MARTINI
(about 1285-1344)
The Annunciation: the
Virgin. - Assissi,
(Basilica di San Francesco)

SIMONE MARTINI (about 1285-1344) - A Miracle of St. Agostino Novello. - Siena, Sant'Agostino

SIMONE MARTINI (about 1278-1344) - Guidoriccio da Fogliano. - Siena, Palazzo Pubblico

PIETRO LORENZETTI
(known from 1305-1348)
St. Francis. - Assissi,
Basilica di San Francesco

PIETRO AND AMBROGIO LORENZETTI

With Pietro and Ambrogio Lorenzetti the Golden Age of Sienese painting of the Fourteenth Century came to an end. They were brothers, worked during the same decades, and it is known that, at least once, they undertook an important work together, *The Histories from the Life of the Virgin*, which they painted as a fresco on the facade of the Church of the Annunciation, or Santa Maria della Scala in Siena. This work which became a model, also through its iconography, for several generations of Sienese painters, fell, however, more and more into disrepair, until finally it was totally destroyed in the Eighteenth Century. Both painters developed and formed their style with complete independence from Simone Martini, but they show the unmistakable influences of the contemporary Florentine trend. The stylistic results to which they came, however, can not be compared; they are intimately connected with the characteristics of each of the brothers.

Pietro who was perhaps a few years older than Ambrogio, had a decided dramatic temperament. In his early work he was influenced by Duccio, but he adopted themes that were more archaic than we find with Duccio and filled his figures with an intense solidity, which seems to bring out his painting in clear contrast to the Sienese tradition. In one of his first paintings, the earliest of his works which have come down to us, a *Madonna with Child*, which was originally in the Dome of Cortona and is now in the Diocesan Museum, the forms are massive and concentrated, without any decorative loosening, the chiaroscuro is strongly marked and depressing, the composition is divided into clearly shown planes and takes up the whole space of the painting which recalls the massive division of planes of a Romanic relief. This serious, firm and strict construction of the forms and space, however, does not exclude emotion, but seems to be created for this very purpose, to give expression, in the sphere of shy intimacy and intensive and hidden passion, to a feeling of a new humanity which animates the characters. Pietro Lorenzetti uses here, for the first time in painting, the touching theme of a mute dialogue of the eyes between the Virgin and the Christ Child; this motif, which was taken from the sculpture of Giovanni Pisano, is often repeated in his subsequent paintings. We find it in a *Madonna* in the Uffizi, a painting of almost Giotto-like solidity, the date of which is uncertain; it is dated by some 1315, by others 1340. We find this theme in the center picture which Pietro executed at the order of Bishop Guido Tarlati for the rectory of Arezzo. His highest perfection, however, is reached in a small fresco in the Chapel of St. Francis in Assissi, depicting the Virgin and Child in half-figure between St. Francis and the Evangelist John, a fresco that we are here reproducing in separate parts.

Here we find for the first time in Italian art the omission of the traditional isolation of the pictures arranged on the same plane which are not connected by any historical event; this was done under the pressure of the emotion, which the artist intended to infuse into each figure. Pietro himself had strongly emphasized the ecstatic hierarchy by placing the figures in the corresponding fresco over the Orsini Tomb in the same basilica, under the ornate arcades of a Medici loggia; but here the isolation is diminished through the shy intimacy of pious conversation and the transition could not have been executed with greater delicacy or more beautiful reticence. The three figures, the Virgin and the two Saints, are clearly separated and removed, but the intervening space is mysteriously animated and lyrically transfigured by the crossing glances and the significant force of the barely suggested words. The Virgin looks silently at her Son and points with the thumb of her right hand toward St. Francis, who humbly and lovingly awaits the blessing by the inexperienced little hand of the Child; the Evangelist, with a dignified gesture, seems to explain the scene.

In the same Assissi church Pietro left his greatest fresco cycle, depicting the *Passion of Our Lord*. Its dating is much debated and it is certain that assistants or pupils collaborated; but a grandiose *Crucifixion* in which there appears a swarm of figures and which seems to move to and fro in perspective, is certainly by the master's own hand, as is the *Descent from the Cross* with its complicated, pyramid construction. The sliding of the emaciated body of Christ is of an incisive and exciting linear structure as on the relief of Giovanni Pisano, and is rightly considered one of the highest expressions of the dramatic genius of the Fourteenth Century in Italy. And of equal or even greater moving intensity are the other frescos of Pietro, notably the damaged *Crucifixion* which he painted around 1331 for the chapter hall of San Francesco in Siena, and which was taken in the last century into the inside of the same church; or the *Slaughter of the Innocents in Bethlehem* in Dei Servi in Siena; in the same place we also find several *Histories from the Life of St. John the Baptist* and the *Life of John the Evangelist* which unfortunately are in bad condition and have been partly painted over.

This monumentality of the proportions and the large scale of the concept, worthy of a fresco, we also find in several panel paintings of Pietro Lorenzetti. Besides the ones already mentioned, we might point out the very characteristic altar painting which he executed in 1329 for Del Carmine in Siena and which is now in the City Museum, and above all its center piece on which are depicted the *Mother of God and the Child Between St. Nicholas of Bari and the Prophet Elias with Four Angels*; also the *Birth of the Virgin*, of 1342, now in the Dome Museum of Siena. [In the latter work it is remarkable how the artist boldly broke through the traditional decorative scheme of the triptych after which the painting is externally formed and merged the center picture with the one on the right in one single scene. Apparently he intended to create with this a concrete space and a concrete depth in which he could place the massive monumental forms of his figures of which the two nurses, who at the right witness the eventus, form an excellent example. Their serious religious concentration does not contradict the select surroundings, an aristocratic living room which is enlivened by colored tissues and light-colored draperies. It is thoroughly characteristic of Pietro's art that he knows how to combine his feeling for monumental and strongly outlined masses, in which he is somewhat influenced by Giotto, with his joy in select and minute descriptions; in this he almost anticipates certain phases of Flemish painting.] The above mentioned festive altar painting in the Church del Carmine is supplemented by a predella with *Five Scenes from the Lives of the Carmelites*, a veritable masterpiece, the style of which, in its peculiar manner, is characteristic of so many works of the Siena school. We reproduce in this volume a detail of this superb predella with the representation of the *First Mythical Eremite from Mount Carmel at the Magic Wall of the Prophet Elias*. It is especially worth noting how the figures of the serene and calm, pious monks in their characteristic black and white striped mantles and the curious geometrical form of the well completely harmonize with the lustre of some small details of the surroundings and of the utensils, for example with the multicolored marble decorations of the border of the well, and the little pail with the sheen on its edge.

These little scenes have an almost magical charm; they seem to form a graceful and idyllic interlude in the fiery absorption of the serious and pensive inspiration of Pietro; in this they constitute the nearest approach of his art to the painting of his brother Ambrogio. The latter, however, had an entirely different nature.

Ambrogio's personality was indeed more complicated and more problematical; he was anything but a man of instinct, he was rather a sensitive thinker and a rational being. This did not prevent him from achieving the highest poetical effects in those works in which he entered thoroughly into intellectual examinations, or in which his inspiration seemed spellbound by programmatical or symbolical intentions, in short by demands which lay outside of artistic considerations. This is noticeable in his best known fresco cycle, the *Allegories about the*

Results of Good and Bad Governement, which was painted between 1357 and 1359 in the hall of the *Palazzo Pubblico* in Siena.

It consists of an extensive imagery with political, didactic and moral background, which is unique of its kind and merits for this reason the highest historical and documentary interest. In this cycle the complicated didactic and allegorical disguise does not, however, lessen the artistic effect and the free development of the formal language which is perfectly coherent in its style. In fact the allegory *per se* becomes poetic material. In the *Allegory of the Good Governement,* for instance, symbolized by a magnanimous king, who sits on his throne surrounded by the Virtues, we see twenty-four councillors united by two ropes showing their reverence for the ruler; the ropes constitute a pun as rope, in Italian *corda,* signifies concord or harmony and it is shown floating under the scales that Justice holds above her. The clarity of the composition is remarkable; it develops in a continuous circular rhythm; the personification of the Virtues is likewise admirable; among them we find the famous Peace, a female figure (*pace* in Italian is feminine) whose plastic forms are loosened in a calm rhythm, and who in this most effective and direct way gives lyrical expression to her moral attributes. But even more sublime and more impressive is the mood of the great composition on the adjoining wall which depicts the *Results of Good Government in the City and in the Country.* The main protagonist in this painting is the landscape; an urban landscape in which towers, palaces, balconies and loggias are crowded together and a rural landscape as one can imagine it in the immediate environs of the city, with crossing roads, with occasional castles and farms, with a terrain divided into allotments, fields, vineyards, olive trees and, as in the surroundings of Siena, broad spots of naked rock. No pleasing ideal, nor a picturesque wilderness, but merely every-day peasant land, the scene of hard and happy human labor. Ambrogio notices for the first time the existence of such a landscape which lacks the consecration of a poetical and rhetorical tradition, and seizes its lyrical quality in harmony with the concrete humanity which lives in it. He takes it as it is, in the multiplicity of its aspects. But his representation is never prosaic or literal because he is eager to capture in his pictures as much of the universe as possible and he thereby widens the perspective markedly upward where a very fine strip of sky appears between the ramparts of the towers and palaces or extends over the hills and plains; through this the aspects become magically changed. The city becomes a block of multicolored masses full of edges and windings, the land becomes a wonderful unreal carpet with light and dark spots. The human beings move between them with that nonchalant grace of the clay figurines which stand out from the fairytale-like background of Neapolitan mangers — maidens dancing in the squares, masons laboring on the roofs, horsemen riding out to hunt, promenading ladies, artisans working in their shops, peasants going to market, reapers, vintners and wanderers — all these figures resemble flowery parables in an oration which mirrors with eloquent colors the customs, the patriotism, the hopes and the fears of that social order which had developed in the free urban communities of the most civilized regions of the Italy of the Middle Ages.

With equal sagacity Ambrogio succeeded in portraying the empty and dissolute elegance of the *jeunesse dorée* of his time, in the ludicrous groups of courtiers who attend the solemn *Admission of St. Louis of Toulouse into the Franciscan Order*, in his fresco in the Church of San Francesco in Siena. At one time his desire for knowledge even induced him to depict curiously gowned Mongolian and Tibetan types in his fresco *Martyrdom of the Franciscans in Ceuta*, which in the same church faces the afore-mentioned fresco. Ambrogio's mental activity shows in his interest in all possible aspects of the culture of his time; with a sense that one could almost call pre-humanist he even renewed some classical Graeco-Roman themes but he sought, above all, the most difficult problems of artistic expression and searched for new artistic solutions. He was the only artist of the Fourteenth Century who, clear-sighted and consistant, carried out research in perspective; this is shown, in addition to the frescos about good government, in several panel paintings, among them an *Annunciation* of the year 1344 in the Siena Museum, in which for the first time all lines of the composition converge in one point. His figures convey the impression of materiality by an entirely new method, almost without using a chiaroscuro, as was done by Giotto, but through an intimate connection between zones of pure colors and the tense, elastic modeling of the contours which summarize the forms and identify them in their circumscribed color planes.

We owe to the delicate, well thought-out and constant application of these principles everything that constitutes the magic and the originality of Ambrogio's work; that feeling of a serene superhuman absorption which his paintings radiate and which finds its expression in that ideal of blossoming and voluptuous female beauty which he venerated. An unforgettable example of this can be found in the wonderful *St. Dorothea* in the Siena Museum. We can recognize that avoidance of the dramatic and of movement which, however, does not lead to coolness and indifference toward these sacred themes. It induced him repeatedly to express the most fervent and incredibly delicate emotions of motherhood in a series of *Madonnas* in which the motif of a dialogue which Pietro loved so much, is replaced by a tender embrace, the blending of Mother and Child; we might remember the enchanting youthful *Nursing Madonna* in the seminary of Siena where the low-bent profiles are so absorbed and so blended in each other that they embrace zones of the liveliest pure colors. It is that mirror-like transparency which, in the fresco of the good government, breaks up the palaces and fields into innumerable color spots, gives to the towers and walls of the city by the sea a crystalline sharpness or modulates the calm surface of the inlet by the reflection of the mountain on the shore.

The two little paintings in the Siena Museum are unique in the painting of the whole Fourteenth Century; they are not just fragments or backgrounds of a larger figure composition but isolated and pure landscapes which in their almost metaphysical loneliness without sky are filled with a poetry hard to define.

The two brothers Lorenzetti died probably in the year 1348, victims of the plague which at that time visited all of Europe. If, as has been said appropriately, Sienese painting died of the plague, it is certainly true that with the death of the two Lorenzettis, four years after Simone Martini, eleven years after Giotto and twenty years after Duccio di Buoninsegna, the Golden Age, the almost mythical language of the greatest geniuses and the strongest personalities of Italian painting of the Middle Ages found its end. In the second half of the century there was nobody who could compare with the greatness of these old masters.

PIETRO LORENZETTI (known from 1305-1348) - Madonna and Child. - Assissi, Basilica di San Francesco

PIETRO LORENZETT
(known from 1305-1348)
St. John. - Assissi,
Basilica di San Francesc

86

PIETRO LORENZETTI (known from 1305-1348) - The Carmelite at the Well. - Siena, Museum

PIETRO LORENZETTI
(known from 1305-1348)
The Birth of the Virgin:
the Nurses. (Detail)
Siena,
Museum of the Dome

88

AMBROGIO LORENZETTI
(known from 1319-1347)
M a d o n n a.
Siena, Archepiscopal Seminary

AMBROGIO LORENZETTI
(known from 1319-1347)
St. Dorothea.
Siena, Museum

AMBROGIO LORENZETTI (known from 1319-1347)
The Admission of St. Louis of Toulouse into the Franciscan Order. (Detail). - Siena, San Francesco

AMBROGIO LORENZETTI
(known from 1319-1347)
The Good Government.
Market Scene.
Siena, Palazzo Pubblico

AMBROGIO LORENZETTI (known from 1319-1347) - View of a City. - Siena, Museum

AMBROGIO LORENZETTI (known from 1319-1347) - Port at the Sea. - Siena, Museum

INDEX

LIST OF ILLUSTRATIONS

BIBLIOGRAPHY

GENERAL WORKS

G. VASARI, *Le Vite de' più eccellenti pittori, scultori e architetti* (ed. Milanesi, Firenze, 1878-85; ediz. Ragghianti, Milano, 1949).

G. B. CAVALCASELLE - J. A. CROWE, *A History of painting in Italy*, London, 1864 (ediz. ital., Firenze, 1886).

R. VAN MARLE, *The Development of Italian Schools of Painting*, The Hague, vol. I, 1923, e vol. II, 1924.

P. TOESCA, *Storia dell'Arte Italiana*, vol. I, Torino, 1927; vol. II (*Il Trecento*), Torino, 1951.

E. CECCHI, *I Trecentisti senesi*, Roma, 1928.

P. TOESCA, *La pittura fiorentina del Trecento*, Bologna, 1929.

K. WEIGELT, *La pittura senese del Trecento*, Bologna, 1930.

C. H. EDGELL, *A History of Sienese Painting*, New York, 1932.

L. COLETTI, *I Primitivi*, vol. I (Dall'Arte Benedettina a Giotto), Novara, 1941; vol. II (I Senesi e i Giotteschi), Novara, 1946.

G. SINIBALDI e G. BRUNETTI, *Pittura italiana del Duecento e Trecento* (Catalogo della Mostra Giottesca del 1937), Firenze, 1943.

R. OERTEL, *Die Frühzeit der Italienischen Malerei*, Stuttgart, 1953.

GIOTTO

F. RINTELEN, *Giotto und die Giotto - Apokryphen*, Leipzig, 1912; II ediz., München, 1926.

C. CARRÀ, *Giotto*, Roma, 1924.

E. CECCHI, *Giotto*, Milano, 1937.

T. HETZER, *Giotto*, Frankfurt am Main, 1941.

P. TOESCA, *Giotto*, Torino, 1941

L. COLETTI, *Gli affreschi della Basilica di Assisi*, Bergamo, 1949.

DUCCIO DI BUONINSEGNA

C. H. WEIGELT, *Duccio di Buoninsegna*, Leipzig, 1911.

C. BRANDI, *Duccio*, Firenze, 1951.

E. CARLI, *Duccio*, Milano-Firenze, 1952.

SIMONE MARTINI

A. GOSCHE, *Simone Martini*, Leipzig, 1889.

R. VAN MARLE, *Simone Martini*, Strassburg, 1920.

A. DE RINALDIS, *Simone Martini*, Roma, 1936.

PIETRO E AMBROGIO LORENZETTI

E. MEYENBURG, *Ambrogio Lorenzetti*. Zürich, 1903.

E. CECCHI, *Pietro Lorenzetti*, Milano, 1930.

E. T. DEWALD, *Pietro Lorenzetti*, Cambridge, 1930.

G. SINIBALDI, *I Lorenzetti*, Siena, 1933.